Collins

easy learning

Handwriting
bumper book

Ages 7–9

What can fill a room but takes up no space?

Karina Law

How to use this book

- Easy Learning bumper books help your child improve basic skills, build confidence and develop a love of learning.

- Find a quiet, comfortable place to work, away from distractions.

- Get into a routine of completing one or two bumper book pages with your child every day.

- Ask your child to circle the star that matches how many activities they have completed every two pages:

  Some = half of the activities   Most = more than half   All = all the activities

- The progress certificate at the back of this book will help you and your child keep track of how many ⭐ have been circled.

- Encourage your child to work through all of the activities eventually, and praise them for completing the progress certificate.

- Help your child to rest their pencil in the 'V' between their thumb and index finger; their fingers should be between one and two centimetres away from the pencil tip.

- Introduce your child to the 'starting point' in each activity, where they should first place their pencil or pen on the paper.

- If your child is left-handed, check with your child's school to find out how they teach letter formation; some of the strokes will be made in the opposite direction to right-handed writers.

- The National Curriculum states that children should be taught to understand which letters, when next to one another, are best left unjoined. These are called break letters. Some schools do teach children to join some, or all these letters. Check which handwriting style your child's school uses.

Parent tip
Look out for tips on how to help your child with handwriting practice.

- Ask your child to find and colour the little monkeys that are hidden throughout this book.

- This will help engage them with the pages of the book and get them interested in the activities.

(Don't count this one.)

Published by Collins
An imprint of HarperCollins*Publishers*
The News Building
1 London Bridge Street
London
SE1 9GF

HarperCollins*Publishers*
1st Floor, Watermarque Building,
Ringsend Road, Dublin 4, Ireland

Browse the complete Collins catalogue at collins.co.uk

British Library Cataloguing in Publication Data.

British Library Cataloguing in Publication Data

A Catalogue record for this publication is available from the British Library.

Written by Karina Law
Based on content by Sue Peet
Design and layout by Linda Miles, Lodestone Publishing and Contentra Technologies Ltd
Illustrated by Peter Bull Art Studio, Graham Smith, Andy Tudor and Jenny Tulip
Cover design by Sarah Duxbury and Paul Oates
Cover illustration © Gorelova/gettyimages.co.uk
Project managed by Sonia Dawkins

MIX
Paper from responsible source
FSC
www.fsc.org
FSC™ C007454

This book is produced from independently certified FSC™ paper to ensure responsible forest management.

For more information visit:
www.harpercollins.co.uk/green

Contents

Alphabet practice

Parent tip
Help your child to think of and write another food word for each letter of the alphabet.

1 Read the words below. Some of them have already been put into alphabetical order. Write out the missing words.

honey   rice   spaghetti   muffin   apple
     lemon   bread   waffle   vegetables
orange   kiwi fruit   grapes   cake   yoghurt
     fish   ugli fruit   quiche   nuts
zucchini   doughnut   pizza   toast   jelly
     ice cream   eggs   box of chocolates

a _____

b _____

c _____

doughnut _____

e _____

f _____

g _____

h _____

i _____

j _____

kiwi fruit _____

l _____

2 Write the food words from the box on page 4 next to the correct letter.

m _____

n _____

o _____

p _____

q _____

r _____

s _____

t _____

u _____

v _____

w _____

box of chocolates _____

y _____

zucchini _____

How much did you do?   Activities 1-2

Circle the star
to show what
you have done.

Some   Most   All

Spelling patterns: ow, ou

1 Trace the dotted letters. Then write them out three times.

ow _ow_ _____

ou _ou_ _____

2 Read each word. Then write it out three times.

clown _____

shower _____

towel _____

vowels _____

3 Read each word. Then write it out three times.

mouth _____

pound _____

trousers _____

thousand _____

4 Read and write.

A mouse in the house!

_____

5 Write this poem in your best handwriting.

A little boy went into a barn

And lay down on some hay.

An owl came out, and flew about,

And the little boy ran away.

Parent tip Use the progress certificate at the back of this book to make a reward chart for your child.

6 In the poem above, find two words with OW and two words with OU. Write each word twice below. On the last line, write all four words.

How much did you do?		Activities 1–6

Circle the star to show what you have done.

 Some

 Most

 All

Syllables

1 A syllable is a word or part of a word that makes one separate sound when you say it. For example, panda has two syllables: pan-da. Copy the example below.

pan-da _____

panda _____

Parent tip
Ask your child to write the names of objects around the house, then count the syllables in each word.

2 Build words with two syllables using one syllable from each wall. The first one has been done for you.

gar		dra
	pic	
win		ro
	pla	

cket		net
	den	
ture		dow
	gon	

_____ *garden* _____

_____

_____

_____

_____

3 Join each syllable below to a syllable on a balloon to build a word.
The first one has been done for you.

| plas | neigh | pic | jig | in | rug |

tic

saw

bour

by

nic

sect

plastic

_____

_____

_____

_____

_____

_____

How much did you do?   **Activities 1–3**

Circle the star
to show what
you have done.

 Some   Most    All

9

Months of the year

1

Read and copy. Remember to begin each month with a capital letter.

January _____

February _____

March _____

April _____

May _____

June _____

July _____

August _____

September _____

October _____

November _____

December _____

Parent tip
Ask your child to write a list of family birthdays to help practise capital letters.

2 Complete each sentence. Then write out the whole sentence.

My birthday is in _____ .

_____

Halloween is in _____ .

_____

Bonfire Night is in _____ .

_____

Valentine's Day is in _____ .

_____

My best friend's birthday is in _____ .

_____

The summer holidays start in _____ .

_____

The school year begins in _____ .

_____

How much did you do?	Activities 1-2

Circle the star to show what you have done.

Some

Most

All

Spelling patterns: or, ore, oor

1 Trace the dotted letters. Then write them out three times.

or or _____

ore ore _____

oor oor _____

2 Read each word. Then write it out three times.

torch _____

fork _____

story _____

storm _____

unicorn _____

seahorse _____

3 Read and write.

We read stories by torchlight during the storm.

_____

_____

4 Read each word. Then write it out three times.

snore _____

explore _____

score _____

before _____

more _____

seashore _____

5 Read each word. Then write it out three times.

door _____

floor _____

poor _____

6 Read and write.

After mooring our boat, we set out to explore the seashore.

_____

_____

 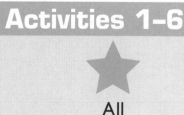

Digraphs: wh, ph

1 Read the wh words. Then write each one three times.

whistle _____

whisper _____

whiskers _____

wheat _____

wheelchair _____

whale _____

whirlwind _____

2 Read the ph words. Then write each one three times.

paragraph _____

trophy _____

telephone _____

phonics _____

sphere _____

3 Read each question word. Then write it out three times.

what _____

where _____

why _____

which _____

4 Read the jokes and copy the punchlines.

Where do you weigh whales!

In a whale weigh station!

What do you call an elephant that never washes?

A smellyphant!

How much did you do?   Activities 1–4

Circle the star to show what you have done.

 Some

 Most

★ All

Spelling patterns: ear, eer

1 Trace the dotted letters. Then write them out three times.

ear   *ear* _____

eer   *eer* _____

2 Read each word. Then write it out three times.

hear _____

fear _____

dear _____

near _____

tear _____

year _____

spear _____

appear _____

Parent tip
Encourage your child to use their non-writing hand to hold the page steady.

3 Read and write.

A bearded knight appeared and killed the fearsome dragon.

_____

_____

4 Read each word. Then write it out three times.

deer _____

steer _____

cheer _____

career _____

5 Read each line. Then write it below.

A cheerful young man from Kashmir

_____

Tried to travel to Rome on a deer.

_____

But the deer veered off course,

_____

At the sight of a horse,

_____

And the young man fell flat on his rear.

_____

Prefixes: re, pre

1 Read these words beginning with re. Then write each one three times.

repair _____

reflect _____

remember _____

repeat _____

reassure _____

reform _____

recreate _____

2 Read these words beginning with pre. Then write each one three times.

prepare _____

pretend _____

prehistoric _____

prevent _____

predict _____

Parent tip
Look for more words beginning with **re** and **pre** in a dictionary, then call them out and ask your child to write them down.

Word endings: tion

3 Trace the dotted letters. Then write them out three times.

tion *tion* _____

4 Read these words ending in tion. Then write each one three times.

information _____

fiction _____

instruction _____

competition _____

addition _____

action _____

attention _____

station _____

subtraction _____

imagination _____

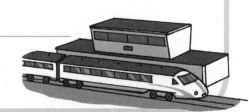

Spelling patterns: oy, oi, ar

1 Read each word. Then write it out three times.

enjoy _____

employ _____

annoy _____

boil _____

noisy _____

disappoint _____

2 Read each word. Then write it out three times.

alarm _____

artist _____

market _____

shark _____

3 Read and write.

The noisy alarm was very annoying.

_____

_____

Compound words

4 A compound word is made up of two other words. Join up the words to make compound words. Then write each one out twice.

milk — corn _milkshake_

fire shake

pop room

class work

life berry

green boat

super way

straw house

gold site

motor market

web fish

Parent tip
Make up rhymes for your child to write down.

Idioms

An idiom is a saying. Read and copy these idioms. Do you know what they mean?

Pull your socks up!

_____

Don't put all your eggs in one basket.

_____

Keep your hair on.

_____

Don't let the cat out of the bag.

_____

Now you've put your foot in it!

_____

Don't count your chickens before they hatch.

_____

Parent tip
Help your child find more idioms from a book or the internet to copy out.

2 Choose a word to complete each saying. Then write the whole sentence.

fly	dogs	bell	cat	cake	book

It's raining cats and _____ .

_____

A piece of _____ .

_____

Saved by the _____ .

_____

Pigs might _____ !

_____

You can't judge a _____ by its cover.

_____

Curiosity killed the _____ .

_____

Similes

We use similes to compare one thing with another. They usually begin with 'as' or 'like'. Draw a line to join the start of each simile to the correct ending.

As proud as a

As gentle as a

As white as

As stubborn as a

As cool as a

As dry as a

As easy as

As fit as a

As wise as an

As quick as a

lamb

flash

pie

peacock

owl

fiddle

snow

cucumber

bone

mule

Parent tip
Find other well-known similes and ask your child to write them down.

24

2 Look again at the similes opposite that you have joined. Write each one in your best handwriting.

_____

_____

_____

_____

_____

_____

_____

_____

3 Complete these two similes in your own words.

My heart is beating like _____

The full moon shines like _____

Proverbs

1 A proverb is a popular saying that teaches a lesson about life. Read the proverb. Then write it in your best handwriting.

Early to bed and early to rise,
Makes a man healthy, wealthy and wise.

_____

_____

_____

2 Read the proverb. Then write it in your best handwriting.

Too many cooks spoil the broth.

_____

_____

3 Read the proverb. Then write it in your best handwriting.

After dinner, sit awhile.
After supper, walk a mile.

_____

_____

_____

4 Read the proverb. Then write it in your best handwriting.

An apple a day keeps the doctor away.

_____

_____

5 Read the proverb. Then write it in your best handwriting.

The early bird catches the worm.

_____

_____

6 Read the proverb. Then write it in your best handwriting.

A stitch in time saves nine.

_____

_____

Parent tip
Write out other proverbs on a piece of paper, with spaces for some of the words. Then ask your child to fill in the missing words.

7 Read the proverb. Then write it in your best handwriting.

Two wrongs don't make a right.

_____

_____

How much did you do? Activities 1–7

Circle the star to show what you have done.

 Some

 Most

 All

Capital letters

1 Capital letters don't join on to any other letters.

Trace and write. Start at the green dot.

A A

B B

C C

D D

E E

F F

G G

H H

2 Trace and write these capital letters.

I I I

J J J

K K K

L L L

M M M

N N N

O O O

P P P

Q Q Q

Capital letters

1 Trace and write these capitals letters to complete the alphabet.

R R

S S

T T

U U

V V

W W

X X

Y Y

Z Z

Around the world

Write a label on each country. Begin each name with a capital letter. Use an atlas if you need to.

France   Spain   Germany   Italy

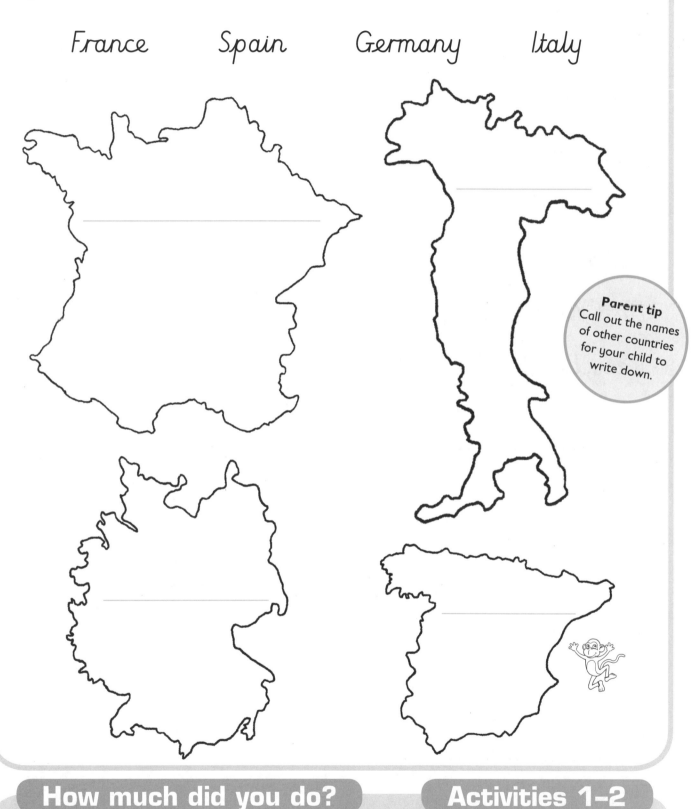

Parent tip
Call out the names of other countries for your child to write down.

How much did you do?

Activities 1–2

Circle the star to show what you have done.

Some

Most

All

Book titles

1 Choose the correct book title to write on each book.
Remember to use capital letters.

The Haunted House by Hugo First

Love and Marriage by Annie Versary

How to Make Money by Jack Pott

Climate Change by Gail Force

Astronomy by I. C. Stars

Bird Watching by Jack Daw

Recycling by D. Sposable

I. C. Stars

_____

_____

_____

Gail Force

_____

_____

_____

Jack Daw

_____

_____

_____

Parent tip
Encourage your child to design eye-catching book covers for their favourite stories.

2 Choose the correct book title to write on each book.
Remember to use capital letters.

_____

_____

_____

Hugo First

_____

_____

_____

Jack Pott

_____

_____

_____

D. Sposable

_____

_____

_____

Annie Versary

How much did you do?   **Activities 1-2**

Circle the star
to show what
you have done.

Some   Most   All

33

More alphabet practice

1 Look at the sports words in the box below. Write the name of each sport twice, in alphabetical order.

athletics   equestrian   polo   volleyball
extreme sports   lacrosse   yoga
ice hockey   diving   netball   orienteering
zorbing   mountaineering   cricket   judo
fencing   swimming   underwater polo
quoits   gymnastics   basketball   karate
hockey   tennis   wind surfing   rowing

a _____

b _____

c _____

d _____

e _____

f _____

g _____

h _____

i _____

j _____

k _____

l _____

2 Write the name of the sport from the box on page 34 twice, next to the correct letter.

m _____

n _____

o _____

p _____

q _____

r _____

s _____

t _____

u _____

v _____

w _____

x _____

y _____

z _____

3 What are your favourite sports?

_____

_____

How much did you do?   **Activities 1–3**

Circle the star to show what you have done.

Some   Most   All

Where is it?

1 The words below are called prepositions. Copy each word three times.

above _____

across _____

after _____

against _____

along _____

around _____

before _____

behind _____

below _____

beside _____

2 Answer the question, using a preposition.

Where is the mouse?

_____

3 Copy each word three times.

between _____

beyond _____

down _____

inside _____

near _____

over _____

through _____

towards _____

under _____

Parent tip
Challenge your child to write clues for a treasure hunt using prepositions like the ones on these pages, e.g. 'Look under a stone'.

4 Answer the question, using a preposition.

Where is the cat?

_____

How much did you do?   ## Activities 1-4

Circle the star to show what you have done.

 Some   Most    All

Spelling patterns: ea (as in head)

1 Trace the dotted letters. Then write them out three times.

ea *ea* _____

2 Read each word. Then write it out twice.

bread _____

head _____

tread _____

spread _____

thread _____

breath _____

heaven _____

breakfast _____

3 Read and write.

I spread jam on my bread for breakfast.

_____

My sister spreads jam on her head.

_____

Vowel sounds: ai/ay

4 Read each word. Then write it out twice.

snail _____

train _____

wait _____

paint _____

play _____

away _____

stray _____

dismay _____

Parent tip
Call out a word and ask your child to write down other words that rhyme with it.

5 Read and write.

I'll stay out of the rain today.

_____

How much did you do?   Activities 1–5

Circle the star to show what you have done.

 Some

 Most

 All

Instructions: How to build a snowman

1 Read these muddled instructions for building a snowman. Copy each one out. Then write the instructions again in the correct order on the opposite page.

Then make a head using a smaller snowball.

_____

Finally, take a photograph of your snowman.

_____

Next, use stones to make eyes and a mouth.

_____

Add a carrot for a nose.

_____

Roll a large snowball to make the snowman's body.

_____

Push sticks into the snowman's body to make arms.

_____

Give your snowman a hat and a scarf.

_____

How to build a snowman.

1 _____

2 _____

3 _____

4 _____

5 _____

6 _____

7 _____

Parent tip
Find other lists of instructions, such as recipes, for your child to copy out.

How much did you do?   Activities 1-2

Circle the star to show what you have done.

 Some

 Most

 All

Word endings: able, ible

1 Trace the dotted letters. Then write them out three times.

able   able _____

2 Read these words ending in able. Then write each word twice.

table _____

vegetable _____

enjoyable _____

suitable _____

believable _____

valuable _____

breakable _____

reasonable _____

fashionable _____

reliable _____

3 Trace the dotted letters. Then write them out three times.

ible *ible* _____

4 Read these words ending in ible. Then write each word twice.

horrible _____

terrible _____

edible _____

sensible _____

invisible _____

5 Read and write.

The raw vegetables were inedible.

_____

Building words

1 Some words are made of two separate parts that have their own meaning. For example, television is made of two parts. Copy the example below.

tele-vision _____   television _____

2 Build words with two parts, using one part from each wall. Then write each word out twice. The first one has been done for you.

tele		auto
	tele	
micro		mini
	mini	
micro		tele

chip		phone
	vision	
graph		matic
	scope	
mum		ature

television _____ television _____ television _____

_____

_____

_____

_____

_____

_____

3 Look at the prefixes in the box. Choose a prefix to add to each of the words below to build a new word. Then write out each word in full.

| auto   tele   photo   mini   micro |

_____phone   _____bus   _____phone

Parent tip
How many other words can your child find in a dictionary that begin with these prefixes?

_____graph   _____graph

_____

_____

_____

_____

How much did you do?   Activities 1–3

Circle the star to show what you have done.

Some

Most

All

Synonyms

1

Synonyms are words that are similar in meaning.

Read the synonyms in the box. Then write a synonym next to each word.

---

small   simple   discover   scream   watch
guess   litter   start   giggle   mistake   repair

---

rubbish _____

estimate _____

shout _____

easy _____

begin _____

laugh _____

find _____

observe _____

little _____

error _____

mend _____

Antonyms

2 Antonyms are words that are opposite in meaning.

Read the antonyms in the box. Then write an antonym next to each word.

> near   wrong   subtract   confident   unsure
> poor   above   clever   worst   arrive

Parent tip
Help your child to think of words that have opposites. Ask them to write down the words, then to write the opposite next to each word.

add _____

far _____

certain _____

below _____

rich _____

foolish _____

depart _____

shy _____

best _____

right _____

How much did you do?   Activities 1–2

Circle the star to show what you have done.

   Some

   Most

   All

Shortened forms

1 An apostrophe is sometimes used to show where letters are missing in words. Write these words out in full. The first one has been done for you.

isn't → is not

wasn't → _____

couldn't → _____

wouldn't → _____

shouldn't → _____

doesn't → _____

haven't → _____

hadn't → _____

didn't → _____

aren't → _____

don't → _____

can't → _____

2 Write the shortened form of these words. Remember to use an apostrophe. The first one has been done for you.

I have → I've

we have → _____

I will → _____

you will → _____

I am → _____

you are → _____

they are → _____

3 Read and write.

I'm afraid we can't board the plane because I've forgotten the tickets!

_____

_____

How much did you do?   Activities 1–3

Circle the star to show what you have done.

Some

Most

All

Word endings: ly

1 Trace the dotted letters. Then write them out three times.

ly *ly* _____

2 Read these words ending in ly. Then write each word twice.

slowly _____

quickly _____

usually _____

smoothly _____

roughly _____

wisely _____

recently _____

excitedly _____

3 Read and write.

The tortoise moved slowly and steadily towards the finish line.

_____

_____

4 Read these words ending in ly. Then write each word twice.

happily _____

sadly _____

loudly _____

quietly _____

silently _____

hopefully _____

thoughtfully _____

successfully _____

5 Read and write.

The frog hopped happily after the fly.

_____

_____

Word search

1 The names of ten musical instruments are hidden in the grid below.
Find and circle each word. One has been done for you.

r	e	c	o	r	d	e	r	s	l
p	l	v	i	o	l	i	n	m	k
o	h	e	e	s	e	s	y	d	e
r	w	p	m	f	l	u	t	e	y
g	b	i	u	e	g	g	j	h	b
c	l	a	r	i	n	e	t	w	o
f	c	n	d	d	a	y	u	c	a
a	m	o	f	h	i	s	b	m	r
g	u	i	t	a	r	b	a	g	d
z	e	j	q	m	t	s	x	w	y

Parent tip
Help your child to think of and write down the names of other musical instruments.

52

2 Write out each musical instrument you have found in the grid three times. Remember to join the letters correctly.

violin   *violin*   *violin*

Collective nouns

A collective noun is the name given to a group.

Copy each example neatly.

A pride of lions.

_____

A pack of wolves.

_____

A swarm of bees.

_____

A flock of sheep.

_____

A crowd of people.

_____

A herd of elephants.

_____

A colony of ants.

_____

A gaggle of geese.

_____

A brood of hens.

_____

More than one: Irregular plurals

2 Not all plural words end in s! Plural words that do not end in s are called irregular plurals.

Copy each irregular plural next to its singular partner.

> *men   children   people   teeth   women*
> *geese   mice   deer   sheep   feet*

sheep _____

tooth _____

foot _____

goose _____

deer _____

child _____

person _____

mouse _____

man _____

woman _____

How much did you do?   Activities 1-2

Circle the star to show what you have done.

 Some   Most   All

55

Word endings: sion, ssion

1 Trace the dotted letters. Then write them out three times.

sion *sion* _____

2 Read these words ending in sion. Then write each word twice.

decision _____

vision _____

occasion _____

explosion _____

confusion _____

conclusion _____

tension _____

mansion _____

3 Read and write.

The noise of the explosion caused a lot of confusion.

_____

_____

Parent tip
Using a dictionary or the internet, help your child to find more words that end with **sion** and **ssion** and write them out.

4 Trace the dotted letters. Then write them out three times.

ssion *ssion* _____

5 Write ssion at the end of each word. Then write the whole word twice.

*se*_____

*mi*_____

*impre*_____

*discu*_____

*percu*_____

*permi*_____

*profe*_____

*proce*_____

6 Read and write.

The percussion instruments made the biggest impression during the procession.

_____

_____

Homophones

1 A homophone is a word that sounds the same as another word but has a different spelling pattern. Homophone is a Greek word meaning 'same sound'.

Join up the homophone pairs. Then write them out. The first one has been done for you.

hair	some	*hair hare*
leak	whole	
son	leek	
two	buy	
hole	threw	
right	hear	
knew	hare	
through	write	
knight	new	
flower	meet	
by	pear	
sum	night	
meat	flour	
here	too	
pair	sun	

2 Underline the homophone in each joke. Then write out the jokes in your best handwriting.

What do you say to a sheep on its birthday?
Happy birthday to ewe.

_____

_____

What fruit never gets lonely?
A pear!

_____

_____

What insect runs away from everything?
A flea.

_____

_____

Why did the other animals ignore the pig?
Because he was a boar.

_____

_____

How much did you do?   **Activities 1-2**

Circle the star to show what you have done.

 Some

 Most

 All

Handwriting practice: 'Nobody loves me'

1 Copy these poem verses in your neatest handwriting.

Nobody loves me,
Everybody hates me,
I think I'll go and eat worms.

Big fat squishy ones,
Little thin skinny ones,
See how they wriggle and squirm.

_____

_____

_____

_____

_____

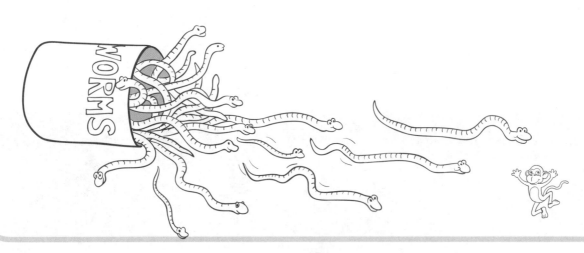

2 Copy the rest of the poem in your neatest handwriting.

Bite their heads off.
'Schlurp!' they're lovely,
Throw their tails away.

Nobody knows
How big I grows
On worms three times a day.

Anon.

_____

_____

_____

_____

_____

Parent tip
Read the poem out loud with your child when they have copied it out.

How much did you do?   **Activities 1–2**

Circle the star
to show what
you have done.

Some

Most

All

Practice pages

1 Use these pages to practise your handwriting. For example, write your own story, letter, poem or description.

Title: _____

_____

_____

_____

_____

_____

_____

_____

_____

2 Continue your writing and draw a picture in the green box to accompany it.

The End

How much did you do? **Activities 1–2**

Circle the star
to show what
you have done.

 Some   Most   All

63

check your progress

- Shade in the stars on the progress certificate to show how much you did. Shade one star for every ⭐ you circled in this book.
- If you have shaded fewer than 20 stars go back to the pages where you circled Some ☆ or Most ⭐ and try those pages again.
- If you have shaded 20 or more stars, well done!

Collins Easy Learning Handwriting Ages 7–9 bumper book

Progress certificate

to

name _____

date _____

pages 4–5	pages 6–7	pages 8–9	pages 10–11	pages 12–13	pages 14–15	pages 16–17	pages 18–19	pages 20–21	pages 22–23	pages 24–25	pages 26–27	pages 28–29	pages 30–31	pages 32–33
⭐1	⭐2	⭐3	⭐4	⭐5	⭐6	⭐7	⭐8	⭐9	⭐10	⭐11	⭐12	⭐13	⭐14	⭐15
pages 34–35	pages 36–37	pages 38–39	pages 40–41	pages 42–43	pages 44–45	pages 46–47	pages 48–49	pages 50–51	pages 52–53	pages 54–55	pages 56–57	pages 58–59	pages 60–61	pages 62–63
⭐16	⭐17	⭐18	⭐19	⭐20	⭐21	⭐22	⭐23	⭐24	⭐25	⭐26	⭐27	⭐28	⭐29	⭐30